embrace

30 DAYS TO LOVING OTHERS WELL

LIFEWAY
GIRLS|
DEVOTIONS

publishing team

Director, Student Ministry
Ben Trueblood

Manager, Student Ministry Publishing
John Paul Basham

Editorial Team Leader
Karen Daniel

Writer
Nikki Tigg

Content Editor
Stephanie Cross

Production Editor
Brooke Hill

Graphic Designer
Kaitlin Redmond

Published by LifeWay Press®

ISBN 978-1-0877-4415-5
Item 005831803
Dewey Decimal Classification Number: 242
Subject Heading: DEVOTIONAL LITERATURE / BIBLE STUDY AND TEACHING / GOD

Printed in the United States of America

Student Ministry Publishing
LifeWay Resources
One LifeWay Plaza
Nashville, Tennessee 37234

table of contents

intro

Love can be a tricky thing—and loving those who are different from us is another matter entirely. We've seen movies with popular girls who run the school and are considered the standard for beauty and what's cool. Sadly, true, godly love for others isn't always something we see elevated as "good." And if it is, it often seems that showing love for others is more about making ourselves look good than doing good for the other person.

God's love should completely change the way we look at love—and the way we see those who are different from us. The ancient Greeks had many words for love, with each one carrying a different idea, implication, and understanding. The Greek term for a love of others is *phileo*, which is often called "brotherly love." (Or, "sisterly love," if you will.)

If you have siblings, you know those relationships can be difficult. Some siblings are super close, even if they get on each other's nerves sometimes. Others are distant or rarely get along. But when God calls us to love one another with *phileo* love, He's asking us to love our neighbors with the same kind of love He poured out on us.

This means that no matter what race, culture, or belief system the girl next to you might belong to, God created her and loves her deeply. Whether you're BFFs or not, you're called to love this girl just like God loves you. Over the next 30 days, we'll examine exactly how we can do that—with God's help, of course.

Our world today is incredibly divided over race, and our goal in this study is to learn what God's Word says about people of other races and to seek to love them as we love ourselves. God is calling us to embrace the girls around us as His beloved daughters—no matter what they look like. We pray that you will begin to understand who God is, how He loves all people, and how we can learn to love all people, too.

getting started

This devotional contains 30 days of content, broken down into sections that answer a specific question about loving others well. Each day is divided into three elements—discover, delight, and display—to help you answer core questions related to Scripture.

discover

This section helps you examine the passage in light of who God is and determine what it says about your identity in light of that. Included here is the key passage, focus Scripture, along with illustrations and commentary to guide you as you study.

delight

In this section, you'll be challenged by questions and activities that help you see how God is alive and active in every detail of His Word and your life. You'll be guided to ask yourself about what the passage means for your relationship with God.

display

Here's where you take action. Display calls you to apply what you've learned through each day's study.

prayer

Each day also includes a prayer activity in one of the three main sections.

Throughout the devotional, you'll also find extra articles and activities to help you connect with the topic personally, such as Scripture memory verses, additional resources, and quotes from leading Christian voices.

day 1

GOD LOVES EVERYONE

discover |

READ JOHN 3:16.

For God loved the world in this way: He gave his one and only Son, so that everyone who believes in him will not perish but have eternal life.

If you've been in church for even a short amount of time, odds are you've heard this verse often. It can be so easy to breeze over this verse, but consider what it means and to whom it applies.

God so loved the world—not just the U. S. or Israel. Isn't that amazing? This Scripture doesn't disqualify anyone—not one person. He loved the world—not just the girl who makes the right choices, not just the girl who always obeys her parents, not just wealthy people, and not just one ethnic group. He loved the world so much that He gave His only Son to die in our place, taking on the sin of the entire world. God revealed the depth of His love by sending Jesus so that those who believe in Him will have eternal life.

Eternal life? What a gift! The magnitude of this gift is overwhelming but think about the Giver of the gift. Think about what this gift cost God. God loves all people so much that He gave His only Son so that all people might have the gift of eternal life. Our human minds can't even comprehend that type of love, and because of that, it can be easy to forget the reality and greatness of God's love for all people.

delight |

Read the key verse. How does it impact the way you see yourself?

How does it impact the way you see others?

Do you find yourself looking at other girls and thinking they are not worthy of God's love? If so, how does this verse challenge you or change you?

display

What are ways you can remind yourself of God's love for all people? Take a moment to write John 3:16 on a sticky note and place it where you'll see it daily or set a reminder on your phone.

God made the first move by loving you and giving up His only Son for your sins. How can you make the first move today by being loving and showing generosity to someone around you?

> We are called to share the truth with all people—not just those who look like us. *Ask yourself: Do I lean toward only sharing with people who look like me?* As you examine your heart, ask God to show you how you can show His love with the people around you who might be of a different race or culture.

day 2

ALL IN GOD'S IMAGE

discover|

READ GENESIS 1:26-27.

Then God said, 'Let us make man in our image, according to our likeness. They will rule the fish of the sea, the birds of the sky, the livestock, the whole earth, and the creatures that crawl on the earth.' So God created man in his own image; he created him in the image of God; he created them male and female.

Every person has been created in God's image. You were created in His image on purpose and for a purpose. There's no one else on earth like you—your hair, eye, and skin color were intentional by God—but what makes you special is that you were created in His image. We often look at others and qualify or disqualify them based on their outward appearance, but this verse is a reminder of what is true—every single person has equal significance and worth and has been made in the image of God.

Here's the truth: God created ALL people in His image, so none of the people He created are seen as superior in His eyes. We often have trouble seeing beyond and understanding cultural differences. This can impact the way we treat others, but the great news is that you don't have to understand another culture to understand that they were created in God's image. God created us all in different shades, which points to His creativity and shows what brings Him glory (Isa. 43:7)

delight |

All people were equally made in God's image, yet not all people are treated equally. How have you witnessed this in your life?

Think about a time you felt left out of your friend group—did you feel lonely, sad or angry? Explain.

Imagine how a girl who looks different may feel when she is left out. Remembering how you felt being left out. How can remembering how you felt when you were left out change the way you treat others moving forward?

display

Sometimes in our society, people of different ethnicities aren't befriended or become outcasts simply because their culture isn't dominant or understood. Have you ever looked at another girl and only focused on your differences instead of similarities? Why or why not?

Do you find joy in knowing you were made in the image of God? Take a moment to think about that reality.

Your friends, strangers, and even your enemies were created in God's image. How does this shape the way you think about and pray for them?

Jot down a short prayer of praise for all the different ways God created us to reflect Him.

day 3

ON PURPOSE, FOR PURPOSE

discover|

READ EPHESIANS 2:10.

For we are his workmanship, created in Christ Jesus for good works, which God prepared ahead of time for us to do.

> **Spend time thinking about how this verse applies to you and ask God to give you eyes to see that all people have been intentionally created on purpose and for a purpose.**

God doesn't make mistakes, which means no one is an accident! Every person has been created ON purpose and FOR a purpose. There was an intent and purpose for every single person to be created. God's creativity is mind-blowing! He created the sun, stars, mountains, and beaches—yet He still knew the world needed you. His creation isn't complete without YOU! He carefully and purposefully created you so that you can do the good things He has planned.

The same way He knew the world needed you, He knew the world needed the girl who sits behind you in science class, the friend you go shopping with, and the girl working the drive-thru at your favorite fast food place. God has a unique assignment for each person He made.

If you are a Christian, three things are true about you. God had good things planned for your life long ago, you have been created in Jesus, and you are His workmanship. The same is true for all believers who are white, Hispanic, Asian, black, and so on. God has a plan and purpose for each person living on this earth.

Sometimes we let opinions, news stories, social media, or gossip cloud the way we see and relate to others—especially those we don't have a lot in common with. We have to remember the truth: God has a plan and purpose for each person on the earth today.

delight |

Personalizing and speaking God's word out loud is a great way to shift the way you see and understand the Bible. Repeat Ephesians 2:10 out loud and include your name in the space provided: For _____ is his workmanship, created in Christ Jesus for good works, which God prepared ahead of time for _____ to do.

Take a moment to think of a girl who looks completely different than you. Now, repeat Ephesians 2:10 aloud and include her name in the space provided: For _____ is his workmanship, created in Christ Jesus for good works, which God prepared ahead of time for _____ to do.

display

Challenge yourself to recognize the image of God in those you encounter this week. Intentionally talk to a girl you might normally avoid.

day 4

JESUS' SACRIFICE IS ENOUGH

discover|

READ HEBREWS 10:11-14.

But this man, after offering one sacrifice for sins forever, sat down at the right hand of God. — Hebrews 10:12

> **Spend time in prayer thanking God for the gift of Jesus' sacrifice. Ask Him to remind you of the grace that has been offered to you and to everyone around you.**

Jesus offered Himself once and for all. One time for all people—regardless of their income level, body type, skin color, or the number of followers they have on social media. Jesus' one sacrifice is enough. Under the old covenant, sacrifices had to be made again and again because of sin—and these sacrifices were ultimately inadequate.

Sin has been a problem in the world for thousands of years. Our world is fallen, wicked, and dark. This is a huge problem, but there's a huge solution—Jesus. He offered Himself as a sacrifice, and His offering for us is final and sufficient. For those who turn from sin and embrace in faith the eternal gift that God offers in Jesus, we are His children and invited and welcomed into the family. When another girl accepts Jesus' sacrifice, she becomes part of the family of God. She is now your sister in Christ. We are not to judge or look down on her, but to love and uplift her as members of the same family.

delight |

Do you ever struggle with trying to "earn" your forgiveness as if Jesus' sacrifice wasn't enough?

Read the key verse again. When do you struggle with viewing others as disqualified from being called sanctified and perfected forever? Explain.

What specific ways do you see girls—or yourself—striving as if works and acts of service could earn our place in God's family?

display

In God's family, we don't all look alike, but we are to remember every other girl is valuable and that Jesus offered Himself up as a sacrifice for all people, no matter their background, skin color, or sin habit. The reality is, Jesus didn't hang on the cross longer for them than He did for you—we are all equal in sin and equal in our need for a Savior. Jesus' sacrifice covers the sin of all people for all time, and there are no exclusions.

Do you find it more difficult to see believers who don't look like you as family? If so, what is something you can implement today to remind you of the truth above?

On an index card, write out the words: *Jesus meets me where I am and HE changes me.* Keep this with you as a reminder that only through Jesus can we become a part of God's family.

day 5

discover|

READ EPHESIANS 1:7-10.

He made known to us the mystery of his will, according to his good pleasure that he purposed in Christ as a plan for the right time—to bring everything together in Christ, both things in heaven and things on earth in him.
— Ephesians 1:9-10

> **Take a minute to ask God to increase your awareness of the wisdom and understanding He richly poured out on you. Ask Him to help you understand—at the heart level—the magnitude of His sacrifice for you and others. Ask Him to increase your desire to see and pursue restoration within His church.**

Through Jesus, redemption, forgiveness, and restoration are available to all people. It makes sense, right? God so loved the world that He gave His only Son, He created all people on purpose and for a purpose, and He sent Jesus to forgive and restore us because of our sin. His great love made a way for us be redeemed and forgiven.

We all equally need God's forgiveness; even one sin is enough to separate you from God. But Jesus stepped in and lived the perfect life you couldn't live and restored your relationship with God that sin ruined. Because Jesus did all of this, He is now the uniter of all people. Regardless of skin color, the type of car they drive, or social media influence—all people can be unified in Christ. Because of the riches of His grace, all of our sins have been forgiven and all who come to Him in faith are included.

delight |

God offers this forgiveness and restoration to you if you repent and turn from your sin to follow Him. What does His willingness to do this for you say about His willingness to do this for others? What does this reveal about His love for ALL people?

Where do you see the need for restoration in your life, your family, community, or country? What can you do about it?

display

Because of Jesus' sacrifice, forgiveness and reconciliation are available to all people. No matter how wealthy they are, their skin color, or what neighborhood they live in, there can be unity in Christ. Jesus seeks to unify people. However, in our country—and, unfortunately, some of our churches—there is division over these very things.

What is one thing you can do today to keep these differences from dividing you from others?

List some specific issues that you've seen cause division among girls. Pray that God would strengthen our hearts to seek unity above our own desires.

Once you've seen the need for reconciliation in our country, what steps will you take to be reconciled with people in your school or community this week?

day 6

A CALL TO LOVE

discover

READ JOHN 13:34-35.

'I give you a new command: Love one another. Just as I have loved you, you are also to love one another. By this everyone will know that you are my disciples, if you love one another.'

Love seems to be the language of the world. Your favorite song, movie, or TV show probably talks about love. Think about it: messages of love are everywhere—including the Bible! However, the world's view of love and God's view are different. The world's view of love is temporary and based on feelings, while God's view is based on truth and lasts forever. God is love, and He commands us to love one another.

You are called to love because Jesus loves you. If you consider yourself a Christian, then you are professing that you follow Jesus. When you follow Him, He leads you to love the girl who doesn't dress, speak, or act the way you do.

Let's be honest: you may feel that some people are hard to love, but not one person is unworthy of His love—and we must love who He loves. As you show love, you reflect the love of Jesus to the world. Can you think of something the world needs more than that? You have a great calling and opportunity to love like Jesus!

delight |

Jesus said we should love just as He has loved us. How does God's love for you model the way you are called to love others?

Christians are called to equally love people we have things in common with and those who are nothing like us. When do you find this challenging?

Think of a time when you expected to be rejected and someone showed you love and grace instead. How did that affect you?

display

List three ways the world defines love and three ways God defines love. What are the similarities and differences?

Ask yourself: *Do I find myself showing love to people using the world's definition or God's?*

Verse 34 says Jesus is giving a new command. Although it is a command, it's also an invitation to love others no matter their background, skin tone, or income level. If you choose to reject the invitation, then you are missing out on friendships that could be valuable. Is there someone coming to mind that is different than you that you know you should get to know better? Reach out to her today.

Spend a moment thanking God for His love. Ask Him to show you His heart for those around you and to give you the heart to love them well.

Embrace

day 7

NO FAVORITES

discover|

READ JAMES 2:1-9.

If, however, you show favoritism, you commit sin and are convicted by the law as transgressors. — James 2:9

It's no secret that our world is sinful. There are people hurting because of being discriminated against based on their skin color. You may not realize it but many girls—even girls at your school— are suffering because of the sin of racism. Racism is rooted in hatred, is in direct opposition to the gospel, and should not be supported by those who are believers. Racism degrades someone who is made in the image of God.

Today's passage makes it clear that we shouldn't show favoritism to anyone. This passage warns against favoring rich people over the poor. God's heart is for all people. He doesn't want us to favor anyone regardless of their race, socioeconomic status, or popularity. It's God's will for us to show love and not make judgments about others.

Racism is sin, which points to Satan. Satan comes to steal, kill, and destroy (John 10:10). What better way for him to try to destroy the church than by dividing it? Racism has divided the church, which is the body of Christ. A body can't fully function if it's divided. As members of the church body, we have work to do.

delight |

Read James 2:9. Showing favoritism—for any reason—is sin. Pause and let that sink in. What does that reveal to you about how God feels about His people?

Read Galatians 3:28-29. We are all one in Christ—you and other believers around the globe. How does this truth affect the way you view others?

display

James said favoritism "dishonored the poor" (v. 6). Dishonor means shaming others or even damaging their reputation; honor indicates respect. How have you dishonored girls who are different from you? What can you do to honor others instead?

Read 1 John 4:20. We can't claim to love God and not love His children. Write down three ways you can show love to a girl who doesn't look like you.

Talking about racism isn't comfortable, but it is necessary.
- If you know girls who are regularly affected by racism, write out their names and pray for them.
- Reach out to these girls and ask to hear about their experiences with racism.
- Continue praying for each girl and ask God to open doors for you to be able to share His love with them—whether they're Christians or not.

Racism is a heart issue. Ask God to search your heart and show you ways that you have unknowingly supported racism. Confess racism as sin and ask God to help you see and love His people the way He does.

day 8

DIFFERENCES AND DIVISIONS

discover|

READ GALATIANS 3:27-29.

For those of you who were baptized into Christ have been clothed with Christ. There is no Jew or Greek, slave or free, male and female; since you are all one in Christ Jesus. And if you belong to Christ, then you are Abraham's seed, heirs according to the promise.

Scripture is clear: Christians have differences. This includes cultural differences, which is an issue in our country and our churches. People tend to divide over visible differences and often side with people who look like them. Think about games you've seen played at school or church; if there is a competition where it happens to be a guy versus a girl, the girls typically cheer for the girls and the guys cheer for the guys. While there is nothing wrong with friendly competition, it is wrong to treat people poorly because of their differences. Paul shared that those differences don't matter because we are all one in Christ. We are all children of God because of our faith in Jesus. No one is less than in God's family—every person is loved, treasured, and equal.

Unfortunately, we see the opposite played out in society. But Christians are called to be different and to treat everyone equally. Treating someone poorly because they are a different race, gender, or materially poor is sin. This sin has to be addressed so that God can bring the healing we so desperately need. Christians can't uphold any form of discrimination, racism, or superiority because Jesus paid the price for each and every person with His life. So, we should treat all people equally.

delight |

Read Romans 2:11. Does this verse challenge or support your beliefs?

How would the world change if we treated each other as image-bearers who are equally loved and made in God's image?

display

Think about how the Bible describes God's care for and Jesus' treatment of the marginalized. List some ways you can model your response to those who are different from you after what Scripture portrays.

We live in a world that is aching from the wounds of unequal treatment. As a Christian, you have the answer. You have the opportunity to love those around you. List three ways God can use you to be a blessing to a girl who is treated unequally.

> **Spend a moment thanking God for the equality we have in Jesus. Confess the ways you have treated people wrongfully and ask God to help you see others as part of His family.**

day 9

GOD CALLS US TO LOVE OTHERS

discover

READ MARK 12:28-31.

One of the scribes approached. When he heard them debating and saw that Jesus answered them well, he asked him, 'Which command is the most important of all?' Jesus answered, 'The most important is Listen, Israel! The Lord our God, the Lord is one. Love the Lord your God with all your heart, with all your soul, with all your mind, and with all your strength. The second is, Love your neighbor as yourself. There is no other command greater than these.'

The Bible is one large book with 66 smaller books inside. It contains over 600 commands, and if you were to start reading, it would take 74 hours and 28 minutes to read it straight through.[1] Yet, the whole book can be summed up into one word: LOVE. Of all the commands in the Bible, Jesus tells us which is the greatest in the verses we read today. You and your friends probably don't always agree on the "best" or "greatest." For example, who's the best actress? Who serves the best mocha? Is fruity or chocolate candy better? Not everyone will have the same answer.

For Jesus to tell us the greatest commandment in the entire Bible is a big deal. But, as you can see, the command is actually two commands—love God and love others. We have to recognize the importance of the order. It's impossible to love others well if we don't first love God.

We often fall short of showing love to others, especially when we disagree or misunderstand each other. We honor God by loving Him, and we must love others no matter what they look like or how different they are from us.

delight |

Think about how much information is in the Bible, and yet, Jesus sums up the most important commands in verses 31-32. What kinds of things do we allow to complicate these instructions?

Take a moment and be honest with yourself about how you live out Mark 12:28-31. Are there any changes you should make? If so, what steps can you make toward those changes?

display

You can show someone love by noticing them. Make someone feel loved and welcomed by inviting a new girl to sit at your lunch table today.

Create a lock-screen for your phone that says: *Live loved, live love.* Let this serve as a reminder that when we love God and live out of His love for us, we can truly love others well.

Spend a moment reading the key passage again. Ask God to help you desire Him and honor Him by loving others well.

day 10

A GLIMPSE OF HEAVEN

discover|

READ REVELATION 7:9-10.

After this I looked, and there was a vast multitude from every nation, tribe, people, and language, which no one could number, standing before the throne and before the Lamb. They were clothed in white robes with palm branches in their hands. And they cried out in a loud voice: Salvation belongs to our God, who is seated on the throne, and to the Lamb!

Do you ever try to imagine what heaven looks like? Today's key Scripture gives a glimpse inside, showing us there's a massive crowd from every nation and every language.

Imagine you're standing before the throne of God, worshiping God with believers from every nation. It's clear that God wants all people to be united in heaven. Many churches today gather and sing praises to God, but oftentimes all the people in the church look strikingly similar. This doesn't reflect what will happen in heaven.

God's vision for His church is bigger than we often settle for. This image of heaven reminds us that while the church is made up of different ethnicities, genders, song choices, languages, and traditions, what we share in common is bigger than our differences. We often focus on the differences, but we can cultivate unity out of our similarities—starting with the fact that we are created in God's image and reflect Him as our Creator.

delight |

Read John 3:16. Write out the words *God loves the world*. Sometimes we try to shrink Scripture down to our view. Sometimes we live like the Scripture says, "for God so loved other girls who look like me." He loves and values people from all nations. One day in heaven, you may be worshiping next to a Chinese man or a woman from Uganda.

Examine your heart: Do you feel comfortable attending church with people who don't look like you? Why or why not?

Read Acts 2:1-12. Why do you think God allowed each person to hear in their native language? What does that tell you about God's heart for people of

all nationalities?

display

In the end, all races will be represented in heaven. How does this affect your perception of what heaven will look like? How does it affect your view on worship here and now?

List two things you can do today to start or improve your friendships with people from other races.

> **Read the key Scripture again. Set a timer for 90 seconds and sit silently to imagine what you just read. Take a moment and thank God that He loves all people. Ask Him to give you a heart to see and celebrate others who don't look like you.**

There is no Jew
or Greek, slave
or free, male
and female;

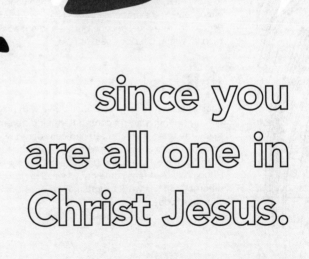

since you are all one in Christ Jesus.

GALATIANS 3:28

day 11

DIFFERENT BY DESIGN

discover|

READ 1 CORINTHIANS 12:14-26.

But as it is, God has arranged each one of the parts in the body just as he wanted. And if they were all the same part, where would the body be? As it is, there are many parts, but one body. — 1 Corinthians 12:18-20

God arranged His body of believers uniquely and on purpose. Your body is made up of different parts and is dependent on each part to work effectively. What do you feel when your body doesn't work effectively? You experience pain. God's design for the church is for us to work together—as one body—and not against one another. Discord within the body causes pain.

delight|

Sports like softball and volleyball thrive with players that are different. When players contribute their different abilities to the team, the team is celebrated and considered well put together. Imagine how a coach feels when she sees the team members building one other up and giving high-fives for points scored. Huge crowds of fans come out to watch a group of players with different abilities work together. How does that relate to our churches today?

Imagine God is the "coach" who hand-picked His team and is eager to see the team use its differences to work together. Consider our churches today. Do you think God is pleased with the way His "team" treats one another based on its differences?

Take a moment to imagine God's team of believers. Each "player" has different spiritual gifts, strengths, backgrounds, and skin color, which God specifically designed. How could a team with such unique "players" unify, working together toward a common goal?

display

Diversity was God's idea, yet many of us don't embrace it. There's a level of awkwardness and misunderstanding when it comes to learning about other girls who look different from you. Name one thing about a girl who is different from you that you've come to realize is a wonderful thing.

Thank God for His intentionality in creating every person. Ask Him to give you the heart to see and celebrate diversity and not reject it.

day 12

CARRYING BURDENS

discover |

READ GALATIANS 6:2.

Carry one another's burdens; in this way you will fulfill the law of Christ.

> **Begin your time today by asking God to give you an open heart and mind to grasp today's reading. Thank Him for the way He has called His people to share their burdens with each other.**

Scripture is to be read and applied. Now that you've read the verse, let's break it down and see how it can be applied.

What is a burden? A burden can be described as a problem someone is experiencing.

What do you do with it? Because of your love for others, you carry or share their burdens, which helps lift weight off of them.

Why? Carrying someone's burden accomplishes the law of Christ. Many people in this country are experiencing the burden of living in inequality. Maybe you've experienced it, or maybe you aren't able to relate. Either way, it's loving to validate the feelings of those who have experienced inequality. Being affected by inequality is a burden that can affect every aspect of a girl's life. It can affect how she is treated in school, the type of college she is accepted to, the quality of jobs she is offered, the type of neighborhood she is "accepted" in, the level of medical care she's able to receive, and so on.

How can you help carry this type of burden? You can help by praying, taking time to listen to her story, and not dismissing it because it hasn't happened to you. You can go beyond liking or sharing a post by reaching out to the person who posted and asking to learn more. This will enable you to hear someone else's experience and better empathize with them.

delight |

Take a moment to truly think about what your life would be like if this was your reality. How would you feel if your skin color or accent caused you to be treated differently on a daily basis?

As a Christian, how do you think you can carry the burden for people who have experienced inequality?

display

Countless people are experiencing inequality, and we are seeing a lot of racial tension in our country. As a Christian, you are not called to ignore it, but to carry the burden of those who are experiencing it. Ask God to give you courage to engage in these conversations.

This will result in uncomfortable conversations, but on the other side of uncomfortable is a step toward unity. Name two girls who have shared with you personally or on social media about experiencing inequality. Contact each girl and ask to hear her story. Take time to listen and pray for and with them.

How do you feel led to speak up for inequality?

day 13

FLIP THE SYSTEM

discover |

READ PROVERBS 22:22.

Don't rob a poor person because he is poor, and don't crush the oppressed at the city gate.

Spend a moment thanking God for how He loves all people. Ask Him to give you eyes to see ways you can speak up for the oppressed and a heart to love people the way He does.

How do you rob a poor person or crush someone who is oppressed? And what is the city gate? What does this all mean?

In today's world, one way to rob or oppress others is through systemic racism. The city gate can be compared to the legal system or company policies. Systemic racism is a way to legally oppress minority races and rob them of the many opportunities given to others. For example, black and brown people have often been unable to receive home loans, which makes them unable to live in certain neighborhoods and attend certain schools. Minority college graduates are less likely to be offered a job after graduation, which limits the diversity of leadership in jobs requiring more skilled labor.

Our country has been and is deeply affected by racism. The reality is that systemic racism affects us all—some people are given superiority, and some are oppressed. However, God doesn't desire for anyone to be superior or oppressed. He loves us all and wants us to treat one another with love and equality, even when it's not popular.

The key Scripture shows how God responds to this type of system; He will champion for the poor and oppressed. He will punish those who put systems in place to rob and oppress others. His desire is love, not oppression.

delight |

Read Proverbs 22:16. How does this verse connect to the key Scripture?

Name other opportunities you think minorities are robbed of and how they experience oppression.

What specific forms of oppression have you seen minority women face?

display

Scripture teaches that racism and oppression are ungodly. Systemic racism may seem like an overwhelming problem. You may be thinking, "What can I do about this? I'm not old enough to change a policy!" No matter your age, you can show love to others who are experiencing a system of racism. How will you show godly behavior in this area today?

Set a timer for 90 seconds to reflect on how racism impacts someone's daily life—even your own. How would you want someone to show love to you? Today, do that for a girl in your life.

day 14

SPEAK UP!

discover|

READ MALACHI 3:5.

'I will come to you in judgment, and I will be ready to witness against sorcerers and adulterers; against those who swear falsely; against those who oppress the hired worker, the widow, and the fatherless; and against those who deny justice to the resident alien. They do not fear me,' says the LORD *of Armies.*

God will come in judgment ready to witness against those who lie, oppress, and deny justice because these things are contrary to His nature. He is a God of truth, love, equality, and justice. God values people and will not tolerate injustice. As His daughters, we must value who and what He values. He values people and justice; we are able to show love to others and honor God by speaking up for those who are denied justice and oppressed.

Throughout Scripture, we see that God cares about injustice, meaning He doesn't desire for anyone to be shown favoritism or be treated unfairly. We are called to be like Him in this pursuit. Maybe you can't reach every girl in the world, but you can reach the girl in your drama class who is treated unfairly by others. Who is the "outcast" in your lunch period? Will you invite her to sit with you and your friends today? When you show love to those who receive undesirable treatment, you are pointing back to the Creator. What an honor and privilege you have to speak up and show love!

delight |

Read Psalm 89:14. Notice what God's throne is founded on. What does this say about how God views justice?

Read Micah 6:8. How should you walk? What do those who walk this way do about injustice?

Read Proverbs 31:8-9. What sticks out to you in this Scripture? What actions do you plan to take as a result?

> **Take a moment to ask God for the boldness to get out of your comfort zone and invite someone different into your space. Repent of any times you may have been "unjust" in the way you have treated people. If you've been treated unjustly, ask God to help you forgive those who have wronged you.**

display

Read Jeremiah 22:3. The first part of this verse says, "This is what the LORD says: Administer justice and righteousness. Rescue the victim of robbery from his oppressor." List the three actions you are to take based on this Scripture. How can you do that this week?

The second part of this verse says, "Don't exploit or brutalize the resident alien, the fatherless, or the widow. Don't shed innocent blood in this place." How are you willing to act on behalf of those who are vulnerable?

day 15

A MATTER OF FAITH

discover |

READ DEUTERONOMY 7:3-4.

'You must not intermarry with them, and you must not give your daughters to their sons or take their daughters for your sons, because they will turn your sons away from me to worship other gods.'

Take a moment to thank God for the truth He gives us through the Bible. Ask Him to give you wisdom and understanding to obey His Word.

Have you been told it is wrong to marry someone outside your race? Some Christians have adopted this idea and use verse three as evidence to "prove" their point.

If you only pay attention to verse three, then it can be taken out of context. However, verse four tells us why God instructed them not to intermarry—it was not because of skin color, but because He knew their hearts would be turned from Him. God loves all people and He desires for people who worship Him to marry someone who worships Him.

The Bible never rebukes someone for marrying outside of their race. Instead, in Numbers 12, God rebukes Aaron and Miriam for criticizing Moses because he married a Cushite (Ethiopian) woman. God even caused Miriam to have a skin disease as a punishment. Interestingly, Aaron wasn't punished in the same manner, but he asked for forgiveness, and forgiveness is only needed when a sin is committed.

Demeaning someone because of their skin color is sinful. God celebrates diversity and does not speak against it, so neither should we. We are called to love all people because God loves all people. We should look at others through eyes of love and not superiority.

delight |

Scripture shows us that God didn't allow intermarriage because of a different faith, not because of a different race. The faith of the person you marry is what matters to God. He doesn't desire for His children to marry unbelievers.

Read 1 Corinthians 6:14. This verse points to the fact that when we marry, we are to marry a believer in Jesus. The faith of your future husband is clearly more important to God than his skin color. Does this challenge or support your beliefs? Explain.

display

Read Romans 10:12. This verse tells us there is no difference between people groups because Jesus is the Lord of ALL. Take a moment to confess to God if you have treated people poorly because of their skin color.

Jesus taught by His actions that we should show love to everyone. How can you speak up against lies about God's Word when it comes to matters of race?

day 16

REJECTING SUPERIORITY

discover|

READ EPHESIANS 2:11-16.

But now in Christ Jesus, you who were far away have been brought near by the blood of Christ. For he is our peace, who made both groups one and tore down the dividing wall of hostility. In his flesh, he made of no effect the law consisting of commands and expressed in regulations, so that he might create in himself one new man from the two, resulting in peace. He did this so that he might reconcile both to God in one body through the cross by which he put the hostility to death.
— *Ephesians 2:13–16*

Do you like winning? We all have a desire to win or be first. While being first can be exciting, it's dangerous to allow our competitive desire to be first impact the way we see and treat others. We are all equal, and there is no superior person or race. God doesn't have favorites, and neither should we.

The reality is that there are people who are treated as lesser because of their skin color. Scripture does not support one group of people being superior to another. God wants His children to be reconciled and tear down the wall of hostility between them through Jesus (v. 16). As Christians, we can't tolerate or justify someone being treated as "less than." Instead, Christians are called to love and walk humbly. Humility and love reject the desire to be superior over others; instead, they acknowledge that Jesus died so that we could all be one in Him.

delight |

Take 90 seconds to find and read John 7:24 and Romans 2:11; 15:5-7. These passages point to the fact that favoring one group or person over another is the opposite of God's will for His children.

Read Ephesians 2:14 again. How can you reflect this truth in your words and actions toward girls who are different from you?

display

List three ways society tells you that you are superior because of your race.

List three ways society tells you that you are inferior because of your race.

Thinking about the Scriptures you read today, what does God say about you and your race? How does this challenge the way you see yourself and treat others?

Confess any thoughts of superiority you may have. If you have been affected by another girl treating you as "less than," take a moment to forgive her if you haven't already. Ask God to give you eyes to see all people equally and through the lens of love.

"I give you a
new command:
Love one another.
Just as I have loved
you, you are also to
love one another.
By this everyone
will know that you
are my disciples,
if you love one
another."

JOHN 13:34-35

day 17

NO PLACE FOR PREJUDICE

discover|

READ ACTS 10.

Peter said to them, 'You know it's forbidden for a Jewish man to associate with or visit a foreigner, but God has shown me that I must not call any person impure or unclean.' — Acts 10:28

Peter walked closely with Jesus for three years. He saw Jesus show love to all kinds of people of various ethnicities and cultures, and Jesus commanded him to do the same. Initially, Peter accepted only part of Jesus' command. He didn't think he was required to love those of a different ethnicity than him.

Peter took great satisfaction in telling God that he followed the rules (Acts 10:14), and yet his heart was holding on to racial prejudice (an attitude or act of viewing other races or cultures as less than our equals). He didn't associate with people who weren't Jewish, but God revealed to him that he was wrong in his actions. Peter turned from his previous beliefs and took steps toward showing love to those from other ethnicities.

delight |

Peter literally walked side by side with Jesus, yet he still had prejudice in his heart. How is it possible for people who have a relationship with Jesus to still have prejudiced tendencies in their heart?

After seeing the prejudice in his heart, Peter changed his way of thinking. What mindset changes might you need to make?

display

To see change in this area, we must be willing to admit prejudice exists. It exists in our country and world because it exists in our hearts. We must make the brave and uncomfortable confession that our hearts hold prejudice. If we don't confess and turn from it, it will always exist. It may affect you directly or it may not, but it is sin that must be identified and rooted out; it has no place in the heart of a believer.

How is God leading you to respond in this moment? This moment is important, but what will you do in the moment you find yourself having a prejudiced thought about someone? How will you apply today's teaching?

Memorize two verses from the list below to remind yourself of how God wants you to respond to any prejudice that may be in your heart.
- Galatians 3:28
- John 13: 34-35
- James 2:1
- Romans 12:3

> **Be vulnerable and ask God to examine your heart and show you any prejudiced thoughts you have. Ask for forgiveness and a heart to love people the way God does.**

day 18

---

discover |

READ 2 CHRONICLES 7:12-22.

My people, who bear my name, humble themselves, pray and seek my face, and turn from their evil ways, then I will hear from heaven, forgive their sin, and heal their land. — 2 Chronicles 7:14

Christians must come humbly to God and turn from our evil ways. We don't like to admit it, but we have sin in our hearts. As we saw yesterday, one sin people struggle with is prejudice. Prejudice affects people in many ways—physical and mental health, financially, social circles, and so on. Minorities can experience it on a daily basis, which causes their lived experience to be quite different and, honestly, quite painful.

You may not realize you have hidden prejudice in your heart that influences how you treat others. Scripture teaches us to examine our hearts and lives for sin, to seek God's forgiveness—and forgiveness of those we've wronged—and root out the sin in our hearts. Prejudice is sin, and when we recognize its mark on our lives, we must repent. We are all equally loved by God.

delight |

Who are the three people you're closest to? On a scale from 1 to 10, how much do you love them? Is there truly even a way to measure your love for them? Of course not! But think about how you would feel if they were treated poorly and hurt by others. Now, think about a girl who has experienced prejudice. She is immeasurably loved by God, the Creator of the universe. How do you think God feels when people He loves and created are treated unfairly because of how He created them?

Looking at 2 Chronicles 7:14, list the actions Christians are called to take.

Bookmark Psalm 139: 23-24 and use it as a prayer to do the continued work of a "heart check."

display

Is prejudice against others common in your heart, family, or church? If so, how can you humble yourself and turn from evil?

Ask a girl you trust—who doesn't look like you—if you do or say things that are racially insensitive. Use this as an opportunity to become aware of issues you may not have known.

> **Write down names of other girls you know personally or on social media who have been victims of racism. Take a few minutes to pray that each girl would know the love of Christ and can forgive and heal from the brokenness that racism has left in our country. Ask God for humility and to show you the prejudiced ways hidden in your heart. Repent of any known prejudice, accept His forgiveness, and ask Him to heal our land.**

day 19

discover |

READ LUKE 10:25-37.

He answered, 'Love the Lord your God with all your heart, with all your soul,
with all your strength, and with all your mind," and "your neighbor as yourself.'
— Luke 10:27

In this Scripture, Jesus shared the famous parable of the Good
Samaritan. The man in the story needed help, but of the three
people who saw his need, only one stopped. The priest and the
Levite were religious people who saw someone in need and did
nothing. They were silent.

Jesus shared this story in response to the question about eternal
life and the definition of "neighbor." We are called to love our
neighbors as ourselves. Love helps, love listens, and love isn't
silent. Showing love means speaking up when we see someone
in need.

It's no secret that there's racial tension in our country. People are
being discriminated against and experiencing inequality on a daily
basis—not just when it's trending on social media. Unfortunately,
there has been deafening silence from the church when it comes
to speaking up about racism—and silence sounds like support.
Ignoring this issue is easier than facing and fixing it, but being
silent is not loving your black and brown neighbors well.

> **Ask God how He uniquely designed you to use your voice
> to speak up for your brothers and sisters in Christ.**

delight |

The man in the parable helped someone in need—helping cost him, and it wasn't convenient. Your salvation cost Jesus His life, and it wasn't convenient. In other words, God wasn't silent when you were in need. How can you honor God by speaking up for others?

display

Silence hasn't served the church well, and we can't pretend as if racial tensions don't exist. Step into the awkward and uncomfortable conversation because your voice matters—no matter what your experience has been.

If you have been a victim of racism, share your story. If you have not been a victim, don't buy the lie that you can't speak up. You can help by bringing attention to those who are speaking out about their experiences.

Read Isaiah 1:17. List the action words in this Scripture. God wants you to act. Silence is not an option. What can you do today to speak out against racism?

Here are a few suggestions to help you break the silence: read and apply Scripture, read articles, or listen to podcasts on this topic. Reach out to a girl of a different race or culture and ask to hear her story. Follow minority leaders on social media to hear their perspectives. Check out the article titled Resources on pages 76-77 for more information.

day 20

CELEBRATING DIFFERENCES!

discover |

READ PSALM 133:1.

How delightfully good when brothers live together in harmony!

> **Take a moment to thank God that He didn't let your differences keep Him from loving you. Ask Him to help you love and celebrate others.**

The family of God includes people from various backgrounds with different languages, traditions, and skin colors. We don't always understand the differences, and we sometimes allow what we don't understand to keep us separated. God's desire is for us to live together in harmony.

God is delighted to see his children doing life together, regardless of each person's background. We can bring glory to God by living together in harmony through listening, learning, and embracing each other despite our differences. We tend to see the challenges of embracing differences and decide it's too difficult, awkward, or uncomfortable, which leads us to tolerating them instead.

- Toleration says "It's ok if people are different." Toleration accepts that we believe in the same God, but choose not to worship together. With that mindset, we usually don't fully engage, or we make others feel like outsiders because they don't follow our traditions.

- Celebration notices a difference and says, "That's amazing! I'd love to know more about your background!"

We should take time to listen and learn about others. There are likely many things we will grow to appreciate—taking us from toleration to appreciation—which makes "celebration" possible. Celebrating other girls points to God's creativity since He's the One who made us look differently.

delight |

We sometimes view the world as "us" and "them" and don't bother to think about our differences in a positive manner. Is it difficult for you to connect with girls who look different from you? Why or why not?

Read Psalm 133:1 again. Who of a different ethnicity can you begin or deepen a friendship with in effort to live out this truth of this Scripture?

display

Here are some practical ways to move from toleration to celebration.
- If you find a person's name difficult to pronounce, don't make fun of them. Take time to learn their name and honor them by saying it correctly.
- Don't make assumptions about someone's lifestyle (food choices, music, home life, sports they play) based on what you may have seen on TV or movies.

Instead of ignoring people's colors, we should acknowledge them. Identify a girl you can talk to this week to learn more about her culture.

What books, podcasts, or social media voices do you primarily listen to? Does your list include any people of color? Seek out different voices to listen to in effort to help you in this area.

day 21

WONDROUSLY MADE

discover |

READ PSALM 139:14.

I will praise you because I have been remarkably and wondrously made. Your works are wondrous, and I know this very well.

> **Take a few moments to confess when you haven't seen yourself or others the way God does. Ask God to help you see clearly and thank Him for His great love for you and others around the world.**

We've talked a lot about love throughout this book. We've concentrated on loving others, but knowing that you are loved is a foundational part of showing love. The Scripture above is absolute truth: You have been remarkably and wondrously made.

Although that's true, it is likely you've experienced hurt, disappointment, loneliness, and fear. May this verse remind you that you are more than those painful feelings. God's Word—not your circumstances—defines you. You were created with intention and not by mistake.

delight |

How have you allowed other girls' voices to influence the way you see yourself and others? What steps can you take to apply God's Word in that area?

Make a list of phrases people use to describe minorities in the US. Do those phrases agree with what God says about them?

Whether you are a minority or not, write out Psalm 139:14 on a piece of paper. You could make a graphic on your computer or try some hand lettering—get as creative as you want! Pray about who God wants you to give this image to. This is a good way to encourage a girl who may hear these negative phrases being said about her. Think of it like this: You have the opportunity to tell her what God says about her.

display |

It is estimated that seven billion people are alive on the planet right now. That's a lot of people! It's fascinating that no two people have the same fingerprint! God truly made you extraordinary and unique. No one else has your hand print because no one can leave a mark on the world like you can. There is a purpose for you and for all people on Earth. How you treat God's wondrously made people tells a lot about the God you worship. God showers you with His love, and you receive it and share His love with others. Here are some ways you can leave your unique print on the world this week by showing love to others.

- Say the key verse aloud. How does it make you feel when you hear yourself speak that verse?
- What can you do to remind yourself of this truth when you go through difficult seasons?
- When have people treated you in a manner that does not reflect God's love? When have you done the same to others?
- How can you change the way you respond to negative treatment and how you treat others based on what you've learned this month?

day 22

A BEAUTIFUL FAMILY

discover|

READ PROVERBS 27:17.

Iron sharpens iron, and one person sharpens another.

> **Thank God for making a relationship with Him possible. Ask Him to grow your love and willingness to reach across racial lines and be sharpened by other believers.**

We are sharpened by godly relationships in our lives. Unfortunately, we typically are "sharpened" only by other girls who look like us because many of us don't have diversity in our friendships. It's understandable that you probably feel more comfortable hanging out with girls who resemble you or share your experiences. However, God's desire for us is to be sharpened by other believers—those who look like us and those who don't. We tend to focus only on the outward differences, but the heart of a white believer in Utah has the same Holy Spirit as the heart of a Hispanic believer in Tennessee.

We have much more in common than we realize; we have been adopted into the same family through faith in Jesus. God's family includes people from different cultures and backgrounds, which is a beautiful thing! For us to be sharpened by our sisters in Christ, we must be willing to learn more about her by building relationships. By doing this, we can better understand, connect, and grow as the family of God.

delight |

The enemy has a plan to divide God's family. When you look at your church, your friends, and your nation, does it seem like the enemy is accomplishing his goal? Why or why not?

Why do you think we immediately notice the differences in each other rather than similarities?

Read 1 Samuel 16:7. What does God look at? If you build your relationships based on what God looks at, how different would your friend group look?

Does your student ministry or small group reflect people outside of your race? If not, how can you change that?

display |

As Christians, we are called to show love to others, and one way to do that is by having relationships with them. Building and growing friendships doesn't happen overnight—it happens bit by bit, one conversation at a time.

Name a girl who is a believer and outside of your race that you can be sharpened by. Send a text inviting her to grab coffee or hang out after school.

Iron sharpening iron isn't a gentle process. Being "sharpened" by a girl from another race might mean enduring some uncomfortable things—like confrontation and/or repenting of sinful attitudes you've held in your heart. Be open to being "sharpened" more and more into the girl God designed you to be.

day 23

SHARE YOUR HEART

---

discover |

READ GALATIANS 6:2.

Carry one another's burdens; in this way you will fulfill the law of Christ.

When we are burdened by something, we often don't share because it involves emotional pain or hurt. We don't always like to show people when we are hurting, but when we are vulnerable with others, we allow them to share our burden. No matter who you are, what you look like, how good or bad your grades are, or how many followers you have, you have likely been hurt or experienced emotional pain that has burdened you.

There are various burdens that girls all around you are carrying; you may be carrying the burden of being hurt by racism. This type of pain can cause you to feel isolated from other races and cause you not to trust, but you take a step toward healing when you share how you've been affected. By doing this, you are allowing others to share your burden. It may be difficult to communicate your hurts, so ask God for the strength to do so. Take off the mask, be honest with another girl you trust, and allow her to see that you're hurting.

delight |

You may be reading this and haven't experienced racism, but how can you be willing to share the burden of another girl who has? You can be a safe place for her to share her hurts and fears.

Can you only share your burden with people who have shared your experience? Of course not! You can share your story with someone who may not be able to completely relate but is still willing to listen and care. The burden you are carrying won't get better in isolation. Who is God putting on your heart that can share your burden with you?

display

When you allow others to share your burden, you are trusting them with your hurts and pain. You are allowing them the opportunity to show you love, compassion, build trust, and strengthen your bond. Why do you think it's difficult for you to share your heart with others?

Read Matthew 11:28. It is understandable that you may not feel comfortable sharing your burden with others at this moment. However, there is a trusted friend who understands everything you are going through and is always available. Jesus understands, loves you, and wants you to come to Him with your burden. Write down what is burdening you and share it with Jesus.

Thank God for the gift of friends who share your burdens. Ask Him to give you courage to share your issues with the girls around you. Thank Him for always being available to listen when you come to Him with your cares and concerns.

My brothers
and sisters,
do not show
favoritism as
you hold on to
the faith in our
glorious Lord
Jesus Christ.

JAMES 2:1

day 24

MOVING FORWARD

discover |

READ MATTHEW 18:19-20.

'Again, truly I tell you, if two of you on earth agree about any matter that you pray for, it will be done for you by my Father in heaven. For where two or three are gathered together in my name, I am there among them.'

Life can be hard. I'm sure you've dealt with overwhelming situations that felt too heavy for you, and the topic of racism may be one of those situations. Many of us have said and thought things about people that dishonored them and God, who created them. We know that racist thoughts are wrong and we know that God forgives us when we sin, but what comes next?

We must do what Jesus tells us to do. He commands His followers to make disciples of ALL nations, teaching them to observe His commands. He reminds us that He is with us. You don't have to go on a mission trip to live this out; you can do this in your community—at school, work, or while you're at your favorite coffee shop.

delight |

Jesus shared which nations are important to Him—all of them! Do you live like other nations besides yours are important? Why or why not?

Create a lock-screen of Matthew 18:19-20. Set it as a background on your phone to remind you to live out God's design to make disciples.

The work Jesus calls us to is ongoing; we never arrive at the point that it isn't necessary to make disciples of all nations. How does His command and promise in Matthew 18:19-20 help you as you navigate racism? What command does God give you? What does He promise?

display

The topic of racism is a sensitive and overwhelming one, and the church has traditionally avoided it. But the church is called to follow Jesus' commands. How can you live out His commands as it relates to people who look differently than you?

It is clear that there are differences in our races, but those differences should not keep us distanced from each other. Racism builds walls between us that God never intended. How can you take a step toward tearing down the "wall" of racism in your community? At your church? In your home? In your heart?

How does knowing that Jesus is with you help you as you live out His commands?

> Take a moment to thank God that Jesus is always with you. Ask Him to reveal himself to you today and to give you the boldness to follow His commands.

day 25

SPEAK OUT

——

discover |

READ PROVERBS 31:8-9.

Speak up for those who have no voice, for the justice of all who are dispossessed.
Speak up, judge righteously, and defend the cause of the oppressed and needy.

Imagine that you're hanging out with your closest girlfriends and a few girls from a different group come over and bully you. She insults you, your family, and makes other remarks that are offensive. You speak up for yourself, but she continues to say hurtful things and finally walks away. Your friends stood there and said nothing. How would that make you feel? Then, you ask them why they didn't speak up, and they respond by saying it didn't involve them or they didn't know what to say. How would this affect your friendship? Would you feel like your friends were showing you love when they stood by while you were hurting and said nothing?

Racism affects many people, yet it often goes unnoticed because the victims of racism traditionally haven't been heard or understood by those who don't experience it. But Scripture directs those who can speak up to do so and to "love one another deeply as brothers and sisters. Take the lead in honoring one another" (Rom. 12:10). Racism does not honor your sister; however, love does. It's the love of Jesus in us that compels us not to be silent about racism. The world can't point to the love of Christ. Christians have the opportunity to do so by speaking out against racism in a posture of love.

delight |

It is possible for a girl to be treated unfavorably on a daily basis simply because of her skin color. Knowing what you know about racism in America, would you be willing to change your skin color? Why or why not?

How do you think people of color feel when believers have the opportunity to speak up for them and don't?

display

We all want to make a difference in our world, right? You have the opportunity to do so by speaking up for others. Love for others compels us to speak up when we see that they are being oppressed or ignored.

What things are you allowing to happen to others that you wouldn't want to happen to you?

It's not enough just to "be nice" and not say racist things. The world will know us by our love, and love is an action word. What actions can you take to help those who aren't being heard?

Ask God for an awareness and sensitivity to racism and the courage to speak out against it.

day 26

LOVE, NO MATTER WHAT

discover|

READ MATTHEW 5:43-45.

'You have heard that it was said, Love your neighbor and hate your enemy. But I tell you, love your enemies and pray for those who persecute you, so that you may be children of your Father in heaven. For he causes his sun to rise on the evil and the good, and sends rain on the righteous and the unrighteous.'

You are called to love the person who despises or hates you. There may be people who hate and mistreat you because of how you look. Other girls may criticize you because of your skin color; your parents may not get hired for certain jobs because of their race; store owners may follow you around in stores because they assume you are a thief; teachers may give you a harsher penalty than girls of a different race—and what does Jesus say to do when people do this? To love and pray for them.

Let's be honest, that is TOUGH to do on our own. But this command reminds us to depend on God's strength, and it pushes us to reflect His loving nature. Jesus acknowledged that there are evil and unrighteous people, but we must trust Him to judge them accordingly (v. 45). His command for you doesn't change just because others act in hateful ways—He desires for you to love, even though it's tough.

delight |

Jesus said to love your enemies and pray for those who persecute you. Take a moment to think about that. Does that feel impossible or unfair? Why or why not?

Why does Jesus say to love and pray for others even though He knows it's tough?

Read Ephesians 6:12. Christians must remember who our real enemy is. Based on this verse, who is the real enemy?

display

Recall an instance when someone said or did something that was offensive and hurt you. How does that offense still affect you today? What are some ways you can apply today's reading to that situation?

Take a moment to write down any offenses that come to mind. One by one, ask God to help you love and forgive the people who hurt you.

Who came to mind when you read Jesus' words about loving your enemies and praying for those who persecute you? Remember these people as you pray today.

- Ask God to help you forgive and replace the feelings of hurt with love.
- Thank Him for the forgiveness you have found in Jesus.
- Ask Him to help you extend love and forgiveness to others—no matter what.

day 27

discover|

READ 2 CORINTHIANS 5:18.

Everything is from God, who has reconciled us to himself through Christ and has given us the ministry of reconciliation.

We needed to be reconciled to God because our relationship with Him was damaged. Because of racial issues, relationships among people are damaged and reconciliation is needed between us, too. God's love for us made reconciliation possible, both with God and with others. Our love for God should compel us to take steps toward reconciliation with unbelievers and across racial lines.

Reconciliation may feel overwhelming, but it's actually quite simple—your math homework is more difficult than this! Here are three recommendations to move toward understanding others. Racial reconciliation is an ongoing process, so completing these steps should be ongoing as well.

Love. Reconciliation is rooted in love. We won't take uncomfortable steps if we aren't motivated by love for others. Scripture also says we will be known as Christ followers by the way we love (John 13:35).

Listen. Take time to listen to another girl's story. Just listen—don't justify or try to give advice. You will likely hear that she is experiencing anger, hurt, and brokenness. This gives you a chance to hear her perspective and give you an understanding of her lived reality.

Learn. Reconciliation is work, and you can't repair what you don't understand. Take time to learn more about the life experiences of minorities by reading, watching documentaries, listening to podcasts or watching videos. Start by looking at resources on pages 76-77.

delight |

We all want to see unity in our country, and unity starts with you—your thoughts and your interactions with others. It's great to do the work of reconciliation, but it's always a good idea to examine our own hearts.

How do you respond—verbally and through body language—to others in public when they speak a different language? Explain.

How do you treat people who have a name you have difficulty pronouncing or wear a hairstyle you think is unusual?

Ask yourself: *Do my reactions honor God?*

If you don't have love for others, be honest with God about it and ask Him to grow the love in your heart for the whole family of God. Thank Him for making a way for you to be reconciled to Him through Jesus.

display

Racial reconciliation is work and will require you to be stretched in uncomfortable ways. Read John 15:13. This may mean laying down your life of comfort or silence and taking the inconvenient but necessary steps to understand someone else's experience. How do you feel led to live out this verse today? Write out one thing you can do in response.

In a journal, write out the words love, listen, learn. Write out the names of any girls you know who are from a different race or culture from you. Then, list as many ideas as you can of ways you can love, listen to, and learn from her.

day 28

ALLY & FRIEND

discover

READ 1 CORINTHIANS 12:24-26.

Instead, God has put the body together, giving greater honor to the less honorable, so that there would be no division in the body, but that the members would have the same concern for each other. So if one member suffers, all the members suffer with it; if one member is honored, all the members rejoice with it.

God desires for there to be no division within the body of Christ. Instead, He wants us to come alongside each other in times of suffering and in times of joy. Right now, many minority members of the church are experiencing difficulties because of racism. Maybe you honestly don't see it or haven't ever been a victim of it. Even if you have not been a victim, you can still apply today's Scripture by having concern for those who are hurting. You get to not only come alongside as an ally or a friend, but as a sister—because we are all family. As a family of believers, we should be the first ones to come alongside our hurting brothers and sisters.

> **You may want to help, but don't know how or where to start. Ask God to increase your awareness of injustice and your love for those who experience it. People of color experience racism in schools, stores, while on vacation, while walking in their neighborhoods, and even at church. Take a moment to sit in their pain. How would you feel if your life was affected in this way? Ask God to help you go do the very thing you would want someone to do for you.**

delight |

No matter your ethnicity, you can be an ally for someone by embracing the uncomfortable and speaking up when you hear a racially insensitive remark or joke. Speak up when a minority is present and when she is not. Why should we speak up for minorities when others use offensive language—even if they aren't there?

How can you grow in your willingness to listen and empathize with others and listen as they share their experiences?

display

Without using social media, what can you do today to show support for a girl who needs it?

What might cause you to be hesitant to become an ally? Write out anything that comes to mind. Then find Bible verses that can help you overcome your resistance.

The Bible is full of wisdom and truth, but that doesn't mean it's easy to align our lives with it. Becoming an ally to people experiencing injustice won't always be convenient or comfortable. You may notice some of your friends and family don't agree with you speaking up for injustice. How will you deal with that?

day 29

discover |

READ COLOSSIANS 3:12-13.

Therefore, as God's chosen ones, holy and dearly loved, put on compassion, kindness, humility, gentleness, and patience, bearing with one another and forgiving one another if anyone has a grievance against another. Just as the Lord has forgiven you, so you are also to forgive.

Today's Scripture shows you how to respond in light of you are—as girls, we always need this reminder! The verse says that you are chosen by God, holy, and dearly loved. You may not always feel that way, and some people may treat you as if you are not any of those things. No matter your skin color or background, one thing is for sure: you have been forgiven and you are called to forgive others. Maybe someone has said terrible things about you because of the color of your skin, the type of hair you have, or the way you pronounce certain words. But no matter what others have done, you are called to forgive.

Racially insensitive comments can deeply hurt and are not easily forgotten. Remind yourself of today's Scripture. The negative comments don't reflect who God sees when He looks at you. He calls you daughter and sees you as chosen, holy, and dearly loved. He knows that people may say hurtful things, but He wants you to forgive them because you are bringing Him glory when you do.

Think about how God has extended forgiveness to you. You are now able to have a relationship with God because of Jesus' sacrifice. We forgive others because we have been forgiven.

Forgive even when it's hard and even when you don't get an apology. Sometimes you have to accept an apology you never receive, but because of your identity as one who is chosen, holy, and dearly loved, forgiving others is possible.

delight |

Reread Colossians 3:12-13. You may put makeup on in the morning, but what else should you "put on?"

What's your identity?

What actions should flow out of that identity? Why might these actions sometimes be difficult?

display

Maybe you have been a victim of racism and maybe you haven't, but God's instruction for us is all the same. How can you be reminded to see yourself the way God does and let that motivate you to forgive others?

Read Matthew 18:21-22. Is there a girl who consistently sins against you? Jot down her name. Based on this verse, what should you do and how often? Beside her name, write out how you can show love and forgiveness to her today.

> If you have been a victim of racism, ask God to help you extend forgiveness. No one is perfect, so also take a moment to ask God to show you any racist thoughts you have, confess them, and ask Him to help you love and honor others.

day 30

LIVING IN HARMONY

discover |

READ ROMANS 12:16-18.

Live in harmony with one another. Do not be proud; instead, associate with the humble. Do not be wise in your own estimation. Do not repay anyone evil for evil. Give careful thought to do what is honorable in everyone's eyes. If possible, as far as it depends on you, live at peace with everyone.

Over and over in Scripture, we see how God wants us to treat our neighbors, friends, and enemies. He wants our attitude to be the same—one of love, honor, peace, and harmony. God's desire is for us to live at peace with everyone—despite our differences. We may have huge differences in opinion, religion, skin color, or other beliefs, but we must love and live at peace, recognizing that each person is made in the image of God.

Too often, the enemy has been successful in magnifying our differences in ethnicity, which has caused conflict between races in and out of our churches. While we cannot control others, we can allow the Holy Spirit to control us. So, as much as you are able to in your ability to influence others, be a peacemaker.

Ask God to heal our country and to use you to bring harmony. Pray that you will live at peace with people from all backgrounds, colors, and popularity levels.

delight |

Read Verse 18 again. What do you think Paul meant by "as far as it depends on you?"

How often are you in control of you? How often are you in control of others?

Do you find it difficult to understand other girls whose outward appearance is different than yours? Do you think not understanding others makes it more difficult to live at peace with them?

"I refuse to accept the view that mankind is so tragically bound to the starless midnight of racism and war that the bright daybreak of peace and brotherhood can never become a reality"[2]
— *Martin Luther King*

display

What thoughts and feelings are you having about today's devotion? Take a moment to write down how you are feeling about where God is leading.

You can't control other people, but you can control your own thoughts, words, and actions. God wants you to do your best to be a peacemaker. What ways can you put that into practice today?

We all experience conflict from time to time, is there someone you're currently not living at peace with? How can you take a step toward peacefully living with that person today?

Embracing Our Uniqueness

Every single person—whether they believe in God or not—is created in God's image. This is called the *imago Dei*. Being made in God's image doesn't necessarily mean we resemble Him physically, though. Instead, the *imgao Dei* means we reflect a more holistic version of His nature into the world through things like our personalities and souls. Basically, all that we are works together to reflect God's nature into the world.

It makes sense that a God who has a multifaceted nature and various characteristics would create people who reflect that, too. Our differences should deepen our appreciation for one another—and for our incredibly creative God— not deepen the divide between us. Our diversity is a beauty to be embraced, not an issue to be erased or ignored.

The church's mission doesn't change based on what's popular or who makes up the church: it's to love God, worship Him, and make disciples. The cool thing is, churches all around the world are doing just that—all while embracing the uniqueness of their own culture. While it might feel awkward to an outsider, we can find common ground in the grace and love of God while enjoying the differences in the ways we worship.

The Book of Revelation clearly lays out that we will all worship together at the feet of our God in eternity (7:9-10). We were made to worship God and to worship Him together uniquely. We have the common ground we need in the God we love, but enjoying our differences is an unfamiliar practice to many of us. So, as we seek to truly embrace one another, let's take a look at some ways various cultures worship God. Maybe we'll even find ways God is calling us to remodel our own worship.

WORSHIP REVERENTLY

In places like Russia, Ukraine, Bolivia, Turkey, and parts of Brazil, the worship is a bit more traditional. The music setup isn't as showy as some of the contemporary church services we might think of. Sharing personal testimony during the service is a normal occurrence and worshipers may spend time on their knees in prayer throughout the service.

In places where conflict and tensions are high, like the Democratic Republic of the Congo, church leaders might pray blessings over those enduring loss or difficulty. They worship through prayer and through showing compassion to the believers in their community. Worshipers in other areas of the world try to find a happy medium of respecting the traditional musical desires of the elderly with the more contemporary preferences of the younger generation—like they do in Nepal.

WORSHIP FREELY

Places like South Asia, Rwanda, Kenya, Malawi, Uganda, Ghana, Thailand, and India are incredibly free in their worship. From the "action songs" of South Asia, to the rhythm and dancing of numerous African countries and India, all of these countries could be considered passionate, lively, vibrant, and absolutely unrestrained in their worship. Movement is a vital part of these worship times of worship, as it is also a key ingredient of the surrounding culture. Some of these services also refuse to set a strict time limit and encourage things like spontaneous prayer or song.[3,4]

What practices of worship does your family or church engage in?

How do these examples of worship across the world encourage you to embrace a different style of worship?

In what ways have these descriptions of worship influenced the way you view the idea of worshiping God?

Embrace

Embracing God's Design
for Loving Others

Our world is filled with fear, questions, self-centeredness, hatred, busyness, and truthiness (living by what we feel to be true and denying the existence of an ultimate truth). It can be so challenging to know what steps to take, which words to say, and what silences to keep so that we can be present and just listen. There are so many things that threaten to divide us, but what we need is love and unity— as Scripture says: "love, … is the perfect bond of unity" (Col. 3:14).

Truthfully, we have to give ourselves some grace as we learn to love well, because not one of us will do this perfectly. But we can lean into God's Word, lean into the Spirit's leading in our lives, and lean into Jesus' perfect example— and we can cultivate a deep and abiding love for all people. Let's answer six basic questions about love to help us see some practical ways to live out a godly love for one another.

WHO
Read Luke 10:25-37.

Jesus addressed this question directly in a conversation with a lawyer in Luke 10. Jesus responded with the parable of the Good Samaritan. It's important to recognize that the Jews despised the Samaritans. This example was intentional. Jesus lifted up the loving actions of a man the religious leaders looked down on. The underlying point Jesus was making, though, is that our neighbor is anyone. We show love to our family and friends, yes, but we also show love to the outcast, the lonely, and the marginalized (Prov. 31:8-9). We show love to people we know and to those we pass by on the street. Just as God loves all people (John 3:16), we are also called to love all people.

WHAT
Read John 13:34.

While the word for love in this passage is agape—God's unconditional love— it teaches us something about the way we love others. We are able to love well because God has loved us and shown us how to love. In this sense, agape and *phileo* are connected, and in certain cases, the words are actually interchangeable. *Phileo*, however, carries the idea of an affectionate, welcoming, friendly kind of love.[5] This is also referred to as "brotherly love." *Phileo*, then calls us to be friendly, to delight in others, and to joyfully serve them as well. When we love others as family, as this word indicates, we also want what's best for them. Brotherly love is often discussed in the Bible relating to biblical community within the church.[6]

WHEN
Read Proverbs 17:17.

We don't just show brotherly love when it's convenient or popular. We love even when we must take an unpopular stand to do so. We love no matter what the people around us think or say. We show love even when others are unkind. We love people when we get along and when we disagree. We love no matter how we're feeling or what's going on in our lives. We love when we have all the time in the world and when we're super busy. We love when we're interrupted and when we're doing nothing at all. We love, we are compassionate, we are friendly, and we are welcoming—at all times.

WHERE
Read Revelation 7:9.

Our ability to show love doesn't change based on which school we go to, which class we're in, which city we're visiting, or which countries our church happens to be mission partners with. True biblical love knows no boundaries of language, socioeconomic status, skin color, intelligence, culture, or religion. Quite simply, we are called to love whoever happens to be wherever God has placed us at that moment.

WHY
Read 1 John 4:19.

Put simply: We love because we are loved. The depth of God's love knows no limit; ours shouldn't either. We were given a love that we didn't deserve or earn. God loves us because His character is loving, compassionate, and kind. We love family because they are family, even when they hurt us or mess up. This is exactly how we should love others. Putting any kind of qualifier on giving love to others—who are people created in the image of God with intrinsic worth and value—is simply unbiblical.

HOW
Read 1 Corinthians 13.

Write out the positive character traits of love listed in this passage.

Now, write out the things love does not do.

What are some practical ways you can live out these qualities in your community?

Focus in on verse 8 for a minute: Love never ends. It's God's love that saves us, and it's God's love that carries us into eternity. Our calling and purpose here on earth is to lead others to know, love, and serve God. But how can we lead people to the God of love if we are not loving like He loves, if we are not representing His love well? While we won't love perfectly the way God loves us, we can be affectionate, friendly, and welcoming toward others—no matter how alike we are.

Resources

Books

The Gospel and Racial Reconciliation by Russell Moore and Andrew T. Walker
Insider Outsider by Brian Loritts
Oneness Embraced by Tony Evans
Advocates by Dhati Lewis
Be the Bridge by Latasha Morrison

Articles

"Race and the problem with apathy" by Trillia Newbell
(*The Ethics and Religious Liberty Commission [ERLC]*, 2016)

"How we can be beautifully distinct in our conversations on race" by Natasha Sistrunk Robinson
(*ERLC*, 2020)

"Learning to listen: Art, race and empathy" by Mike Cosper
(*ERLC*, 2017)

"Why Reconciliation is Worth It" by Jennie Allen
(*JennieAllen.com* Blog, 2019)

Videos

"Religious Liberty and Racial Justice—It All Matters to God" by The Gospel Coalition (*Youtube*, 2017)

"Trillia Newbell on the State of the Race Conversation in the Church" by The Gospel Coalition (*Youtube*, 2019)

"How To Best Engage In The Conversation About Race | Trillia Newbell" by LifeWay Christian Resources (*Youtube*, 2020)

"Racism is Not a Skin Problem, It's a Sin Problem – Robert Smith" by The Gospel Coalition (*Youtube*, 2015)

"How Can We Better Understand Our Hispanic Brothers and Sisters? | Juan Sanchez" by LifeWay Christian Resources (*Youtube*, 2019)

"Practical Ways to Pursue Racial Reconciliation" by The Village Church Resources (*Youtube*, 2017)

"I'm Not Racist; I'm Color Blind." by Darryl Williamson (*TGC*, 2017)

Podcasts

"15 – Why Reconciliation is Worth It with Latasha Morrison" by Made For This podcast (*Jennie Allen*, August 14, 2019)

"BONUS - This Work Starts with YOU with Latasha Morrison" by Made for This podcast (*Jennie Allen*, June 18, 2020)

A Conversation About Racism Between Black and White Christians by Frank Turek (*I Don't Have Enough Faith to Be An Atheist*, June 26, 2020)

Response

Choose at least one of these resources to watch, listen to, or read. Then, take a minute to journal about the way it influenced your thinking about race and reconciliation.

What quotes stood out to you in the resource you selected? Why?

How do you think this study will affect your conversations concerning race moving forward?

Sources

1. "Infographic: You Have More Time for Bible Reading than You Think," November 19, 2018, https://www.crossway.org/articles/infographic-you-can-read-more-of-the-bible-than-you-think/.
2. "The Nobel Peace Prize 1964," NobelPrize.org, accessed December 22, 2020, https://www.nobelprize.org/prizes/peace/1964/king/26142-martin-luther-king-jr-acceptance-speech-1964/.
3. Lauren Reed, "Photos of Worship and Praise around the World," April 6, 2020, https://www.worldvision.org/christian-faith-news-stories/photos-worship-praise-around-world.
4. Rachel Cohen and Andrew Rivers, "Christian Worship Around the World," International Mission Board (International Mission Board, December 5, 2019), https://www.imb.org/2019/12/10/christian-worship-around-world/.
5. "G5368 - Phileō - Strong's Greek Lexicon (KJV)," accessed October 6, 2020, https://www.blueletterbible.org/lang/lexicon/lexicon.cfm?Strongs=G5368.
6. Chad Brand et al., "Brotherly Love," in Holman Illustrated Bible Dictionary (Nashville, TN: Holman Reference, 2015).